My First

A

APPLE

B

BIRD

C

CAT

D

DOG

E

ELEPHANT

F

FISH

G

GRAPES

H

HORSE

I  ICE CREAM

J JELLY FISH

k

KITE

L

LION

M

MONKEY

N

NEST

O

OCTOPUS

P

PARROT

Q

QUEEN

R

ROCKET

S

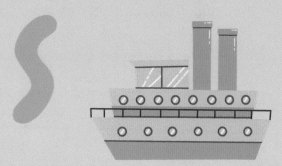

SHIP

T

TENT

V

VAN

WATERMELON

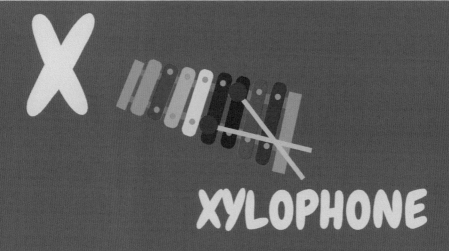

XYLOPHONE

Y

YACHT

Z

ZEBRA

My First 123

1

ONE

ANT

2

TWO

TREES

3

THREE

BALLS

4

FOUR

CAPS

5

FIVE

RAINBOWS

6

SIX

FLOWERS

7

SEVEN

BALOONS

8

EIGHT

COOKIES

9

NINE

BEES

10

TEN

STARS

Printed in Great Britain
by Amazon

22355632R00016